Psychics, seers and oracles tell you what to expect for the next 1000 years!

Original collages by Niki Medlik

James Manning

Prophecies for the New Millennium

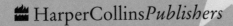
HarperCollins*Publishers*

For my mother and Henrietta Llewelyn Davies

FIRST EDITION

Produced by Thames and Hudson Ltd, London

Library of Congress Cataloging-in-Publication Data
Manning, James. 1948–
    Prophecies for the new millennium: psychics, seers, and oracles
tell you what to expect for the next 1000 years / James Manning
        p.   cm.
    ISBN 0-06-270211-4
    1. Twenty-first century—Forecasts.   2. Prophecies (Occultism)
I. Title
BF1809.M363   1997
133.3—dc21   97-10762

---

97 98 99 00 01 ❖/MK 10 9 8 7 6 5 4 3 2 1

Contents

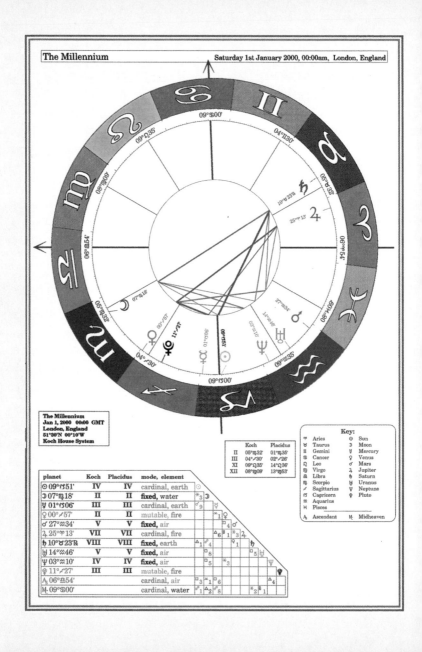

THE WHEEL OF TIME
A Horoscope for the New Millennium

On 1 January 2000, we enter the third millennium of the Anno
Domini calendar, the globally accepted method for the dating of
time. It is the moment when the remnants of the Piscean age are
washed away to bring in the Age of Aquarius, the period that New
Age believers think could lead to the establishment of a Utopia on
Earth. For the majority of people, 31 December 1999 will be the
time to celebrate the past and envision the development of a better
future. It will, without doubt, be a time of great celebration because it
is a very special moment. It is a genuine once-in-a-life-time opportunity to be there at the start of the next stage of our evolution.

However, others think that there is a dark and sinister side to the
advent of the millennium, and prowling through the depths of the
human psyche is a fear that "The End" may come at the beginning of
the year 2000. A subconscious mixing of legend, folklore, rumour,
religion, prophecy and prediction can amalgamate into an all-
embracing fear of extinction, as demonstrated by the rise in the number of millennial cults with apocalyptic visions of the year 2000. Most
notable of late have been the Branch Davidians, whose leader David
Koresh held a firm belief in the approaching "End of the World,"
and the Order of the Solar Temple who also believed that the world
was heading towards oblivion. Both of these groups translated their
vision of the killing fields of salvation into a catastrophic reality.

Prophecies for the New Millennium shares the many visions of our millennial future Believe what you will, but remember that all things are
possible in all possible universes – so greet the New Age with a spirit
of love, hope and understanding .

Starting at the exact moment of the beginning of the new millennium, the chart on p. 6 shows the main features and influences for the first two decades of the 2000s. It reveals that the human race will enter the new millennium in a mood of hope and dynamism. It is a chart that contains plenty of positive aspects and demonstrates the potential for human beings to create a new and better world.

There are more planets in Aquarius – as befits the Age of Aquarius – than in any other sign. They are Mars, Uranus and Neptune. The sign of Aquarius is classically connected with the advance of all things technological and futuristic. However, Saturn is in Taurus and the restraining influence of Saturn – the planet of discipline – means that technology will not take over every aspect of the world. Mercury and the Sun are in Capricorn. Pluto and Venus are in Sagittarius.

The Sun in Capricorn and Moon in Scorpio are in a good and harmonious relationship to each other – a sextile – and will produce an inspiring and balancing energy. Capricorn is also the sign of tradition and likes to work its way into things slowly and solidly, and will act as a balance to the influence of the dynamic, pioneering and innovative planets in Aquarius. Aquarians often think in terms of fifty years ahead of their time, and this balance will mean that the initial decades of the 2000s will retain the best of the old world while embracing the new.

The chart also has polite Libra rising and caring Cancer on the mid-heaven. The two, combined with the Moon's north node in the community orientated eleventh house, suggest a marked improvement in co-operation and understanding between nations. There is a strong indication that all the nations of the world will work together more genuinely than previously and in the true spirit of the friendly Aquarian age.

Venus in Sagittarius is a pointer towards a lot of mixing and relating of different nationalities and races. Marriage would seem to be on the decrease, along with Piscean Christianity. This will lead, in true innovative Aquarian style, to different structures for families.

Aquarius is well known to be an androgynous sign, and there are indications that the new millennium will see more people turning to a gay lifestyle. The square between the ruler of the ascendant (Venus) and the ruler of the descendant (Mars) is a warning to people to continue to put sufficient energy into their personal relationships in an age when work and technology will be very much at the forefront of their mind.

Jupiter, in pioneering Aries, indicates a considerable degree of expansion into new and presently unthought-of areas. Jupiter is also well aspected to Mercury, the planet of brain power and communication, and to Mars, the planet of getting things done on a more concrete level, which is an excellent sign for the New Age.

Saturn in Taurus means that the idea of going back to the land and trying to exist in a self-sufficient way will become even more popular, but the Aquarian age means working together for the good of everyone.

As with all charts, this chart for the 2000s represents a wealth of directions, but it is up to human beings to exploit them.

THE MYSTIC MILLENNIUM
Heavenly Signs of a New Age

For the majority of people, 31 December 1999 will be the time to celebrate in great style their past achievements and to envisage an even better and more fantastic future in the third millennium, as the human race strives to realize its elusive ideals of perfection. Amidst all the celebrations, however, some people will still maintain an unshakeable conviction that the journey and the future are destined to come to a terminal halt on or around 1 January 2000.

The idea of a finite time for the world has a long history. In the third century B.C., the Babylonian astrologer Berossus hypothesized that the universe is eternal but is destroyed every so often by either flood or fire. Ancient Jewish beliefs centered temporally on the concept of the Great Week, which divided history into seven phases. The early Christians adopted this concept because God created the world in six days and rested on the seventh, and each day of his work was equivalent to one thousand years. The adoption of the Anno Domini calendar, created by the Scythian monk Dionysius Exiguous in 525, has therefore made the millennium an especially important date.

The convictions of those who foresee a doom-laden future are often based either upon the writings, forecasts and insights from seers and mystics and lead to a belief in a New Age – or upon a fundamentalist belief in the *Book of Revelation*. These believers are convinced that the signs and portents show that the run-up to the year 2000 is a period that will become ever more apocalyptic and will culminate in either the start of Christ's thousand year reign or in the dawning of a new and more enlightened age.

THE GOLDEN DAWN
1 January 2000

The Sun rises, a golden orb soaring into the sky, casting life-giving rays on the surface of our fragile blue and white planet. It heralds the start of another perfect day for everybody on Earth, but this day is the most special of all days. It is the first day of the first year of the third millennium.

But why is the year 2000 so significant and special in our annals of history and time? It is, after all, only an arbitrary date in the Anno Domini calendar, which is based on an assumed date for the birth of Christ but now dictates the measurement of the world's time and many peoples' expectations for the future. The end of 1999 marks the moment of transformation from the past to the future – the end of the old age and the beginning of the new. The year 2000 is our entry into the unknown, the moment in time in which we have vested our hopes and visions for a new and better world, a stimulus to our own cosmic millennial dreams. Such dreams have been the subject of prophecies and prognostications from seers like Nostradamus to the New Age believers of our own time. Their mystical insights into the future, prompted by the implications of such a crucial date, provide us with a sense of removal from humdrum reality and inspire us with hopes for a time of peace, wisdom and light.

THE COMET PROPHECIES
Nostradamus Foresees Danger

Throughout human history, comets have been considered as portents of divine displeasure and harbingers of doom. The dread they inspire is graphically evoked by the historian Nicetus, who wrote in 1182: "A comet appeared in the heavens like a twisting serpent... lusting for human blood." Ambroise Pare, a famous French surgeon, wrote in awe of a comet in 1582, "The comet was of extreme length and the colour of blood. At its extremity, we saw the shape of a bent arm holding in its hand a great sword as if about to strike us down." Patrick Moore, the distinguished British astronomer, has noted that one reason for the human fear of comets is the apprehension that a maverick may appear out of an ominous astrological sign, such as one of the four fixed signs of the zodiac: Leo, Taurus, Aquarius and Scorpio, which correspond to the Four Beasts of the Apocalypse as described in the Book of Revelation, and head directly towards the Earth. Astronomers, however, are reassuringly of the opinion that this is unlikely to happen.

The opinion of mystics is somewhat different. Nostradamus (born Michel de Nostradame on 14 December 1503 in Saint-Rémy, France), for example, sounded an ominous note with regard to comets in the mid sixteenth century:

"After great misery for mankind, an even greater approaches
When the great cycle of the centuries is renewed.
It will rain blood, milk, famine, war and disease.
In the sky will be seen a fire, dragging a trail of sparks."

(CENTURY 2, 46)

THE GREAT COMET
The Return of a Celestial Sign

The approach to the millennium has already seen an impressive increase in cometary activity. In July 1994, Comet Shoemaker-Levy 9 broke into pieces and smashed into the atmosphere of Jupiter with spectacular effects and Comet Hyakutake was visible in the 1996 night sky. These, however, have only been precursors of the arrival of "The Great Comet," which is making its first appearance in our skies in 3,000 years; it is also known as "Comet Hale-Bopp."

On 23 July 1995, an unusually bright comet, still outside the orbit of Jupiter, was independently observed by Alan Hale in New Mexico and Thomas Bopp in Arizona. It was the most distant comet ever discovered by amateur astronomers and appeared one thousand times brighter than Halley's Comet at the same distance. Comets are normally inert and dark when they are beyond the orbit of Jupiter so, because of its brightness, it was concluded that Hale-Bopp was exceptionally large.

As the comet approaches the Sun, its brightness should increase even more. Currently it is as bright as Sirius, the brightest of all the stars, and anticipation is high that Hale-Bopp will be the brightest "naked-eye" comet of this century, providing a dazzling celestial show for the millennial Earth.

One group, Heaven's Gate, has already committed mass suicide, in California in March 1997, because its 38 members and leader believed that Hale-Bopp was the sign of the arrival of a spacecraft from the "Level Above Human" and that they would be transported to a new realm.

THE GREAT PLANETARY CROSS
Astrological Perspectives in 1999

Comet Hale-Bopp, the celestial messenger, introduces an even more important event: The Great Planetary Cross. This significant astrological conjunction is preceded by the last total solar eclipse of the second millennium on 11 August 1999, ushering in the renewal of the great cycle of the centuries, the end of the Piscean age which has been with us for approximately the last two thousand years, and presaging the start of the Age of Aquarius. An astrological age is the time that the Earth is in a particular sign of the zodiac and is estimated to last for about 2,000 years; it is, however, only a month in the cosmic year, the total of the twelve zodiacal ages. Astrologers considering the future of the Earth will be fascinated by the position of the planets in the four fixed signs of the zodiac. The Sun and Moon will be in Leo, a fire sign, and traditionally the most powerful of the zodiac signs. Leo is associated with great leaders, kings and powerful nations. Mars, the planet of war, will be in its own sign of Scorpio, a water sign. Saturn, one of the most malefic of planets, is in Taurus, a fixed, determined and unyielding earth sign. Finally, Uranus, the planet of dramatic change and revolution is in its own air sign of Aquarius, symbolic perhaps of the dawning of the Age of Aquarius and the start of a new world age.

This heavenly line-up could either exert undue stress upon the planet, causing major planetary changes at the time of the new millennium. Or, it may be considered as a Christian symbol, signifying the imminence of the Second Coming.

The New Age movement first began to make itself felt in the mid and late nineteen-sixties. It combines elements from a wide range of disparate sources and beliefs including: ancient Eastern philosophies, Greek and Roman mythology, Hinduism, Buddhism, mysticism, witchcraft, astrology and science fiction, its very different adherents share a conviction that the "aware" people of the world will experience a shift in consciousness as the world enters the Age of Aquarius, abandons materialism and embraces a new-found spirituality.

Paco Rabanne, fashion designer and now New Age guru, foresees angelic salvation for humanity. A race of extraterrestrial beings called the Elohim (Hebrew for "God" or "of the Gods") were responsible for the creation of the first civilization on Earth – Atlantis – and came to our rescue when Atlantis was destroyed, notably by saving Noah and his family. The Elohim have continued to keep a watchful eye on our development

and may intercede to save humanity again. This latter-day rescue will result in an evolutionary step into the Fourth Vibratory Plane and will be distinguished by a new spiritual understanding, Homo Sapiens becoming Homo Spiritualis. This move to the higher plane will fulfil the Biblical prophecies of the creation of a new heaven on earth.

THE AGE OF AQUARIUS
Hope and Harmony for Mankind

Believers in a New Age have consistently interpreted the prophecies of such seers as Nostradamus as an indication that the dawning of the third millennium will not result in Armageddon but in the golden Age of Aquarius.

This new beginning will mark the end of the Piscean age, which has been an era dominated by the tenets of Christianity. Pisces is the astrological symbol of the fish, and the Piscean values are those of tolerance, empathy and self-sacrifice. Jesus described himself as the "Fisher of Men." The new Aquarian values will be those of friendship, peace of mind, and of contented community living. This New Age will probably be guided by a New World Teacher, just as a new avatar has been introduced to the world every time there has been a significant shift in the collective consciousness.

Silver Birch has been one of the most renowned of twentieth-century North American Indian "spirit guides," speaking through the mouth of trance medium Maurice Barbanell, an editor of Psychic News. He has described the forthcoming age in a collection of his "writings," The Philosophy of Silver Birch: "As our teaching grows in your world, it will mean the end of separateness between peoples. It will mean the end of national barriers, race distinctions, class distinctions, colour distinctions and all the distinctions between churches and chapels, temples, mosques and synagogues. All will learn they have a part to play in the Great Spirit's truth. Out of apparent confusion, the divine pattern will take shape, harmony and peace will come."

NIRVANA OR NOTHING?
What the World's Religions Predict

The year 2000 is a pivotal moment for many of the world's great religions and for New Age believers, who term the current era the "End Time." Many evangelical Christians – born-again, fundamentalist, charismatic and Pentecostal – expect the Second Coming of the Lord. Their generally held belief is that the world was created in about 4000 B.C.; thus, the year 2000 is held to be the start of the "seventh" millennium. It is predicted that at this date Christ will return for his millennial reign as described in the *Book of Revelation* (20:4): "They lived and reigned with Christ a thousand years." The Roman Catholic church has instructed its followers to contemplate the mystery of salvation during the countdown to the dawning of the year 2000.

Although the coming millennium relates to the Christian view of the measurement of time, other world religions also expect significant change on or around that date. The Buddhists expect the Wheel of Dharma, the metaphorical wheel of time, to turn for the first time in 2,500 years. Gautama, the Buddha, taught that each revolution heralds a new beginning for mankind. In this instance, it could signal the advent of Maitreya – the Buddha who is yet to come. The Hindu time cycle known as Kali Yuga, the Age of Iron, the fourth and most depressing of their world ages, is also drawing to an end; the next era should be an Age of Gold.

REVELATION
From Creation to the Final Rapture

The *Book of Revelation* is central to the apocalyptic vision of many fundamentalist Christian sects and cults, mainly because it describes the Second Coming and the Last Judgment. Written by St. John the Divine near the end of the first century A.D., it is his vision of the Alpha and the Omega – the Beginning and the End. For many Christian groups, the "End" is the end of the twentieth century, the end of the final millennium, the current decade the "End Time."

The importance of the year 2000 in fundamentalist Christian beliefs is derived from the definition of "Biblical time." "In the beginning God created the heaven and the earth...And God saw everything that he had made....And the evening and the morning were the sixth day. Thus the heavens and the earth were finished ....and he rested on the seventh day" (*Genesis*, 1:1–31, 2:1). This description of the Creation, however, posed the question of how Biblical time should be dated? The answer came in the *Epistle of Barnabas*, written about A.D. 120. It states, "God finished his work in six days....That means in 6,000 years God will bring all things to completion because for "Him" a day of the Lord is as 1,000 years....In six days, that is in 6,000 years, the universe will be brought to its end."

The next and most crucial question was, when did God create the world? This remained open until 1650, when James Ussher, who became Archbishop of Armagh and Primate of all Ireland in 1654, claimed that the date of the Creation was the evening of 22 October 4004 B.C.

BREAKING THE SEALS
Hope for the Chosen

The breaking of the seals described in the *Book of Revelation* is one of the most fearsome but ultimately joyful forecasts for selected members of the human race. The Lamb of God, Jesus, breaks the seals which bind a great book. When the first seal is broken, a rider armed with a bow emerges on a white horse. He is given a crown and sets out on an expedition of conquest. The second seal brings a rider on a red horse who is given a sword and the ability to make men kill; this destroys all peace on Earth. The third seal sees a rider on a black horse carrying a pair of scales. The fourth seal brings out a pale horse ridden by Death. This apocalyptic figure is given dominion over a quarter of the Earth and the right to kill by war, famine and pestilence. The fifth seal sees the appearance of all those who have been killed for their belief in the word of God (*Revelation*, 6:1–11).

Then, the sixth seal is broken. It is the day of the wrath of God, which is taken by many fundamentalists to describe events that could happen before the dawning of the third millennium: "When he had opened the sixth seal... there was a great earthquake; and the sun became black as sackcloth... the moon became as blood; And the stars of heaven fell unto the earth." It continues with the Angel of the East crying out: "Hurt not the earth... till we have sealed the servants of our God in their foreheads... and there were sealed an hundred and forty and four thousand." (*Revelation*, 6:12–13, 7:3–4).

The chosen 144,000 will be joined by believers from all the other races of the world who survive this great tribulation. Together they will dwell in the temple of God, serving him day and night.

THE SEVENTH SEAL
Beyond Armageddon

"And when he had opened the seventh seal, there was silence in heaven about the space of half an hour." (*Revelation*, 8.1.). When the seal is broken, mass destruction follows: a third of all the world's vegetation is destroyed; a blazing mountain falls into the sea, destroying a third of all sea creatures; the rivers are poisoned and everybody who drinks from them; a third of all the stars are destroyed.

Those who do not have the seal of God upon their foreheads are tormented mercilessly. A third of all mankind is killed, and the Devil sent down to Earth, deceiving mankind into worshipping him and bearing his mark – the number of the "Beast," 666, (later adopted by the English occultist, Aleister Crowley). Those who worship the Beast suffer appalling torments and die in agony, until the time of the battle on the great day of God Almighty at Armageddon – the final victory of good over evil.

After Armageddon, Satan is cast into the bottomless pit for one thousand years, and all those who had died for Jesus and who had not worshipped Satan or received his seal are saved. Then comes the

Day of Judgment, when everybody is gathered before God, and whoever is not marked down in the Book of Life will be cast into the lake of fire for eternity. The survivors inherit a new heaven and earth. There is no more death, sorrow, crying or pain, because the things of the past have all been swept away.

MILLENNIAL DHARMA
The Next Turn of the Great Wheel

The coming of the third millennium also coincides with major events for the followers of Buddhism.

After achieving Enlightenment, the Buddha formulated the doctrine which could be passed on to other truth seekers. This was known as the *dharma*, meaning "law" or "teaching." One of the most potent symbols of the *dharma* is the wheel, emblem of the Buddha himself, expressed by bringing the tip of the thumb and forefinger together, signifying a perfection which has no beginning or end.

Gautama, the Buddha, also spoke of "The Wheel of Dharma" which turns every 2,500 years. Each turn of the wheel brings about a new vision for mankind that slowly comes to fruition, fades away and is followed by another vision of the future. It has been calculated that the next turn will coincide with the dawning of the third millennium. This turn will bring about a new beginning with many changes and new awakenings, possibly even the advent of the Maitreya – the Buddha who is yet to come – and the creation of a new harmony on earth.

THE END OF KALI YUGA
From the Age of Iron to the Age of Gold

Hindu cosmological history is divided into four world ages, each represented by a metal: gold for the first age, Krita Yuga; silver for the second, Treta Yuga; copper for the third, Dwarpara Yuga. Lastly, comes our present age, Kali Yuga, the Age of Iron, calculated to end with the dawning of the third millennium. Happily, the world then returns to the Age of Gold.

Kali Yuga has been a dark age, a "twilight of the Gods;" a period when the "universal truths" have been abandoned. Instead, people have flocked to false prophets whose self-deception has been taken wrongly as a sign of an inner spiritual knowledge. It has been a time when the acquisition of material possessions has been considered preferable to understanding and following the paths of righteousness.

How accurately this description of Kali Yuga summarizes the feelings of so many people as we approach the end of the millennium! An utterance by Krishna from the *Bhagavad Gita* is particularly appropriate in its depiction of a progression towards a promised age of contentment and justice: "At the end of the night of time, all things return to my nature. And when the new day of time begins, I bring them again into the light." The new age of Krita Yuga is forecast to be one in which right will rule supreme, and a sense of well-being will be all-pervading.

QUEEN OF HEAVEN
The New Marian Age of Peace

The concept that we are living in the time of "a world gone bad" is not confined to Eastern religions. It is a view echoed by the Marian author, Dr. Thomas Petrisko, in his book, *Call of the Ages*. Since 1989, he claims, we have been living in a world of confusion and upheaval, the result of the approach of the year 2000. Not only are numerous wars being fought, but nature itself is rising up in revolt against this wicked age in the form of floods, hurricanes, earthquakes, and droughts. These ecological disturbances and wars signify the last days of the struggle against Satan and will end with his defeat at the end of the century.

A vision from the Virgin Mary, received in 1983 by the visionary from the former Yugoslavia, Mirjana Dragicevic-Soldo, is a portent. Satan presents himself before the throne of God and asks to be allowed to tempt the followers of the Roman Catholic Church; God has allowed him this century as the time of temptation, hence the view of many Christians that we have lived under the power of the Devil during the last hundred years. Dr Petrisko, however, believes that the Virgin Mary is guiding the world by her messages to Marian visionaries.

39

ANTI-CHRIST
The Struggle of Good and Evil

God rules in Heaven but the Devil rules on Earth. This simple credo inspires both the traditionally religious and those of a New Age persuasion, as the world approaches the end of the Piscean age. According to one's point of view, the world will either be saved by the Second Coming and enjoy a thousand years of peace, or humanity itself will achieve a higher wisdom and eradicate wars, inequality, poverty and famine.

This view of the end of the twentieth century reflects the belief that Satan has been given this century to lead the followers of the Church away from the path of righteousness. This notion can be traced to Pope Leo XIII (1873–1903), who had a vision of a discussion between Satan and God, in which the former surmised that, given enough time and power, he could overthrow the Church. In response, God gave him the twentieth century as his chance to test the faithful. However, the arrangement was that, at the dawning of the new millennium, this licence would be withdrawn.

Fundamentalist Christians expect the Beast, also known as Anti-Christ, to rule the world just before the advent of the new millennium and many candidates have been put forward for this title, including Saddam Hussein, the late Ayatollah Khomeni, Colonel Gaddafi, and even Bill Clinton. Admittedly, the final two years of this millennium are rich with a dread symbolism: nineteen hundred and ninety-eight is three times the number of the Beast – 666. Nineteen hundred and ninety-nine is even more ominous, since it can be construed as an inversion of the figures 666, together with a figure one, which is the universal symbol of perfection, unity, predominance and beginning.

THE EVIL CENTURY
Is Satan's Reign at an End?

In his *Century 2.10*, Nostradamus referred to the coming of "a very evil century," which the events of the past nine decades have shown to be our very own, more than fulfilling the prophetic warning of the French seer in its two World Wars. Even today, more wars are being fought throughout the world. Religious factions are battling for supremacy. States are exporting terrorism, revolution and intolerance to their neighbours. Famine is prevalent in many parts of the globe, while new plagues and diseases sweep through the world's population. The planet is an ecological time-bomb.

However, there is a ray of hope for everyone who fears that Anti-Christ and the end of the world will both occur by the year 2000. This note of relief comes from an Irish saint writing over 1400 years ago: St. Columbcille (522 – 597), builder of the monastery on the island of Iona. His predictions for the future included the English invasion and occupation of Ireland, the coming of the railway and the emigration of the Irish following the great potato famine of 1845 – 50. But, with regard to the end of the world, we may be assured that it will not occur in the year 2000 because God has promised to "send a deluge over Ireland, seven years before the last day."

THREE DEVILS
Who is the Third?

"And I stood upon the sand of the sea, and saw a beast... having seven heads and ten horns...and the dragon gave him his power...And they worshipped the beast, saying, Who is like unto the beast? who is able to make war with him?...and power was given unto him to continue and forty and two months...count the number of the beast: for it is the number of a man; and his number is six hundred three score and six" (*Revelation*,13. 1 – 18).

The role of Anti-Christ, or the Beast, whose number is 666, is one of the main concerns of apocalyptic millennnarianism; it is thought that he will rule the world for forty-two months before the battle of Armageddon. The concept of the Beast has long fascinated seers and prophets, especially Aleister Crowley (1875 – 1947), the occultist and mystic who had what he described as "a passionate sense of identity with the Beast 666" and who revelled in his reputation as "the wickedest man in the world."

The prophecies of Nostradamus foresaw three attempts by Anti-Christ to subvert humanity; two have already taken place. The first Anti-Christ has been identified as Napoleon, although he was little more than a warm-up act for the truly evil figures of the twentieth century. The second person to claim the mantle of Anti-Christ was Hitler, although Nostradamus named him slightly differently – as "Hister." Fortunately the "thousand-year Reich" was thwarted and is now a shameful part of humanity's history. But there is still a third Anti-Christ to come – and before the end of the millennium, named by Nostradamus as "Mabus."

SAVIOUR OR SATAN?
Anti-Christ in Jerusalem

Jeane Dixon (1918 – 97), popularly known as the "Seeress of Washington," first rose to fame because of her prediction of the assassination of President Kennedy. However, her most astonishing forecast concerns a saviour of mankind who will mutate into Anti-Christ before the dawning of the third millennium. Jeane received this vision of the future of the human race on the 5 February 1962. This date was extremely significant because the original seven astrological planets, the Sun, the Moon, Mercury, Venus, Mars, Jupiter and Saturn were in Aquarius; many people thought at the time that this planetary line-up heralded the Age of Aquarius.

On the morning of that February day, Jeane Dixon awoke to find that the view from her Washington bedroom window had changed from an ordinary street scene to that of a desert at sunrise. In the middle of this desert scene were Queen Nefertiti and the Pharaoh Akhenaten. The royal couple were surrounded by a vast crowd. Nefertiti was cradling a new-born baby whom she presented to the waiting multitude. Before Jeane's eyes, the child grew into a man, and was then surrounded by the entire human race in postures of extreme devotion. She interpreted her vision to mean that a great leader had been born who would unify the world into one all-embracing faith, but the full meaning of the vision would not become obvious until 1999. A few years later, Jeane announced that she had misinterpreted her grand vision and that her "perfect being" was in fact Anti-Christ and would rule the planet from Jerusalem.

PEACE FOR THE CHOSEN
After the Great Tribulation

The Yoido Full Gospel Church of Korea was originally founded as a Pentecostal tent ministry in 1958 by its pastor, Dr David Yonggi Cho. Today, it has a registered membership of 700,000 and is one of the most fervently fundamentalist of the world's Christian churches.

Dr Cho has no doubt that the 1990s and the year 2000 will fulfil the predictions of the *Book of Revelation* on the Second Coming and the great battle of Armageddon. However, the faith that buoys him and his followers is the belief that they will escape the horrors of this time and enter Christ's millennial kingdom.

Cho's vision of the last years of this century and the time of the new millennium sees Anti-Christ established on Earth, while all the members of his own church are transported up to heaven by the Holy Spirit. The rest of the world will experience three-and-a-half years of the "Great Tribulation." During this time, war will break out and destroy the world's cities. At Armageddon, a 200-million-strong Chinese army will do battle with the army of Anti-Christ. Christ will then descend from heaven, to destroy the remnants of the two opposing armies which have united against him. The only people then to enter the millennial kingdom will be those from the Gospel Church, Jews and some chosen Gentiles. At the end of the thousand years, after The Day of Judgment, the redeemed will enter the New Jerusalem, while everyone else is consigned to the lake of fire for all of eternity.

THE FACE OF GOOD AND EVIL
Who is Anti-Christ?

Some modern commentators consider that the Anti-Christ is already among us, and currently biding his time and building his powers before assuming his position of world subjugator. Paco Rabanne, for instance, has identified a 28-year-old man in London, England, as a possible Anti-Christ. Another avatar of the New Age awaiting his hour in London is The Lord Maitreya. His spokesman is Benjamin Creme, born in Scotland in 1922 and a practising esotericist for over 30 years. When speaking at the Friends' House, London, in the summer of 1992, Creme said that The Lord Maitreya has been mistaken for Anti-Christ through a lack of understanding of the *Book of Revelation*, since Anti-Christ is not a man but an energy force. Creme says that this energy force was deliberately unleashed in the distant past and represented the first aspect of God, set free to clear the way for Christianity. The force was last released in the form of Hitler. The Lord Maitreya's message is ultimately one of hope: the Anti-Christ awaited by millions of Christians with Armageddon on their minds will not appear.

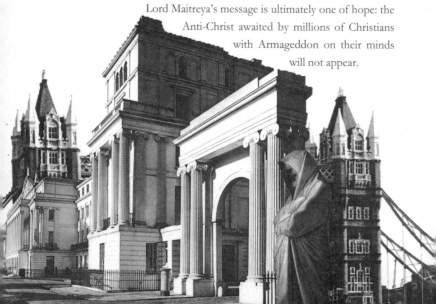

WAITING FOR THE MAN
And Where Is the Child?

Under the influence of an entity he called "The Universal Mind," Edgar Cayce (1877 – 1945), the American seer known as the "sleeping prophet," predicted the destruction of a large part of the globe by 1998, the advent of World War III in 1999, and the end of civilization in A.D. 2000.

One of his most startling millennial predictions came in 1934, when he claimed that a child called John Penniel would be born in America and that this boy would be "Beloved of all men in all places, when the universality of God in the earth has been proclaimed. He will come as a messenger not a forerunner, and give to the earth a

new order of things." This event will occur at a time of the "Darkening of the sun and of several major earth changes."

This child has yet to come to public awareness, but could he be the new world avatar who will guide the world into the year 2000 and the new millennium?

APOCALYPSE AND ARMAGEDDON
The End of a World Gone Wrong?

As the last years of the twentieth century vanish into the pages of history and the new millennium looms, fundamentalist Christians and New Age believers, although two disparate and often antagonistic groups, share a mutual fear: that it could just be the end of the world. As the cycle of time changes to the "seventh" millennium, fundamentalist Christians fear the prospect of Armageddon, while other groups are influenced by the predictions of such seers as Nostradamus whose language often coincides with that of the Bible in describing Judgment Day.

The *Old Testament* warns against the dangers of seduction by false prophets, and there has seldom been a time when there has been such a proliferation of alternatives to mainstream religion. Leaders of various cults have often claimed messianic qualities and then led their followers to murder, suicide and mass destruction.

On a broader front, the nations of the world endure an apparently never-ending stream of internal revolutions and external wars. Dramatic shifts in climatic features have led to famine across large swathes of the globe and to freak weather conditions that have had disastrous consequences for other parts of the planet. This potent cocktail of global abuse, war and rebellion and the worship of religious leaders practising for personal profit is an apocalyptic combination that has led many people to believe Armageddon to be close at hand.

THE BEGINNING OF THE END
Feelings of Millennial Unease

 The world as we know it will come to a natural end because stellar evolution indicates that the composition of the Sun over the course of many billions of years will change. It may even vaporize the entire solar system in one big bang, but this event is so far into the future that the majority of people do not worry about it. Many are much more concerned by the possibility of the end of the world happening in the very near future – in the year 2000. These fears are either based on Biblical prophecies or the forecasts of mystics, and are further stirred by a combination of legend, folklore and rumour.

Of all the mystics who have made forecasts regarding the end of this millennium, few have had the impact and on-going renown of Nostradamus (1503 – 66). He wrote 942 quatrains – four-line verses – which were grouped together in "Centuries." Much of what he wrote is hard to understand and open to wide-ranging interpretation, being composed of symbols, anagrams, metaphors and grammatical tricks. However, Nostradamus claimed that all his prophecies have "but one sense and one meaning," and they have made him famous throughout the world, not least because he forecast that the world would come to an end in July 1999.

THE GREAT PROPHECY OF DOOM
Not Quite The End!

Nostradamus made what is probably the most famous end-of-the-world prophecy ever written:

"In the year 1999 and seven months,
From the skies shall come a great king of terror.
To bring back to life the Great King of Angolmois,
Before and after Mars reigns happily."

(CENTURY 10, 72)

July 1999 is not, then, going to be the start of the summer holidays, but the beginning of the end. But, Nostradamus does leave us with some residual hope:

"There will be a conjunction of Mars and the Sceptre,
Under Cancer, a calamitous war.
A little time after, a new king will be anointed,
Who will bring peace to the Earth for a long time."

(CENTURY 6, 24)

In *The Mysteries of Nostradamus*, Dr. Christian Wollner deduces that the Sceptre represents the planet Jupiter, and that the only time there can be such a planetary conjunction is on 21 June 2002. Chaos and destruction at the turn of the millennium may then be followed by a long era of peace and good will.

JUDGMENT DAY
St. Malachy and the Last Pope

Maul Maedoc Ua Morgair, known as St. Malachy, was born in Armagh, Ireland, in 1095. He became a priest at the age of 25 and was made Bishop of Connor at 30, and later Bishop of Down. He correctly predicted the date of his own death – All Souls Day, 1148 – and became the first Irishman to be canonised in 1190.

In 1139, he traveled to Rome where he presented Pope Innocent II with a list of all future Popes until the end of the world. However, it was not until 1595 that Dom Arnold de Wyon, a Benedictine historian, discovered the list in the Vatican archives and published it. The forecasts are in the form of 112 Latin epigrams which identify all the Popes from Celestine II (1143 – 44), the Pope who succeeded Innocent II, to the last Pope of all. After John Paul II, the list gives only two Popes.

Malachy associated the penultimate Pope with the slogan "Gloria Olivae," meaning "The Glory of the Olive." This could mean that he will be a peacemaker and draw all the different strands of Christianity together. Alternatively, the Benedictines are known as the Olivetans, which could suggest that the next Pope will come from that order. St. Benedict, their founder, once predicted that a Benedictine would become Pope before the end of the world, and that he would lead the forces of Catholicism to a great victory over the forces of evil.

Malachy's last Pope will be "Petrus Romanus," "Peter of Rome," thus demonstrating that the first shall be last and the last first. John Paul II is neither a young nor a healthy man, and if his successor should suddenly die, will Peter of Rome be sitting on the papal throne in time for the Armageddon year A.D. 2000?

WARNING VISIONS
The Marian Messages

Prophecies from the Virgin have on many occasions predicted disaster and retribution for the human race at the time of the new millennium. An example of a doom-filled vision occurred at La Salette, near Grenoble, France, in September 1846. Two children, who were looking after a flock of sheep, saw a beautiful lady wearing a white robe covered in pearls. Around her neck hung a large crucifix with a figure of Christ upon it. At the end of the left arm of the cross was a hammer and to the right a pair of pincers. Weeping, she then spoke to the children: "If my people will not repent, I shall be forced to let go the hand of my Son."

She then warned of various disasters that would take place if humanity did not give up its sinful ways. By the end of 1846, the area of La Salette was completely barren of potatoes, phylloxera struck down the grape harvest, all the walnuts died and a type of cholera which only infected young children had become an epidemic.

The most famous of all Madonna visions took place in 1917 near the Portuguese village of Fatima, about 80 miles north of Lisbon, where the Virgin appeared to three children and confided the Three Secrets, of which the third was the most momentous. It was finally released to the Pope in 1960, and it is alleged that it read: "Fire and smoke will fall from heaven, the waters of the oceans will become vapours. Millions and millions of men will perish and those who survive will envy the dead. But those survivors of all these happenings will proclaim God again and His Glory. They will serve him as in the time when the world was not so perverted." This vision of the Apocalypse coincides clearly with the expectations of many fundamentalist Christians for the forthcoming thousand years.

SUN BEAR
Apocalyptic Messages from Ancient Wisdoms

Sun Bear (1929 – 92) of the Chippewa people was the founder and medicine chief of the 31,000-member Bear Tribe Medicine Society (BTMS). He started their official magazine, *Wildfire*, and wrote many books, including *Black Dawn/Bright Day*, a book of prophecy drawing on both his own and traditional Native American predictions. From an early age, he received visions which reinforced his belief that the neglected wisdom of native peoples had much to teach our technologically orientated and materialistic society.

He found modern man's habits and attitudes threatening to the existence of life on this planet: weather patterns were being changed, increasing the likelihood of natural disasters. His forecast for the millennium is particularly cataclysmic: he was convinced that the earth would erupt in protest, a planetary gesture he likened to a dog shaking itself vigorously to get rid of fleas: "The planet will survive these immense changes because they are necessary for its survival, but millions will die."

He forecast that, before the year 2000, the world's cities would suffer a complete collapse as a result of earth changes. To survive this disaster, "People must change their way of life, retreat to the countryside and develop a much higher consciousness. These changes will be very positive and good for all of creation. It will be the beginning of a new age for those willing to change themselves."

TIDAL WAVES
From Politics to Prophecy

Ruth Montgomery is a contemporary political journalist turned New Age seer. In her book, *Herald of the New Age*, she delivers a message for humanity that intersperses doom and hope at the time of the new millennium.

She predicts that, in the summer or autumn of 1999, the Earth will "flip" on to its side, with the result that the poles will shift to South America and the Pacific respectively. This dramatic movement in the earth's axis will result in the oceans engulfing land masses in gigantic tidal waves. California, the British Isles, the Netherlands and Japan will be especially vulnerable; hurricanes will scour the remaining land.

But there will be survivors, who will prosper by following the basic precepts of New Age: keep to high ground and move out of the cities into the countryside. These survivors will be assisted by the return of people who had been taken to safety, prior to the axis shift, by extra-terrestrials. The return of those saved by the "aliens" will herald the start of the Age of Aquarius, because they will have the new knowledge that will transport the human race on to a new and more powerful plane of human consciousness and enlightenment.

THE SETTING SUN
A Japanese Armageddon

In the view of Shoko Asahara, the leader of the Aum Shinrikyo cult, "The Religion of the Supreme Truth," all societies have "weak links," those who are unenlightened. In this he is in agreement with other New Age prophets, like Sun Bear, urging that it is better to be rid of these human liabilities prior to entering the new stage of wisdom at the year 2000. Unfortunately, Asahara decided to put his views into practice in the form of sarin gas attacks.

Chizuo Matsumoto was born in 1955 and adopted the name Shoko Asahara in 1984. As a young man, he joined Agononshu, a religious movement taught that the purpose of life is the removal of bad karma through Buddhist prayer and yoga. He then travelled to the Himalayas to seek "wisdom." On his return to Japan, he founded Aum Shinrikyo in 1987. Asahara then began to adopt and adapt ideas from Hinduism, Old Testament apocalyptic prophecy and the writings of such mystics as Nostradamus, transforming Aum Shinrikyo into a millennial cult, with himself as its messianic leader.

From 1988, Asahara began to issue instructions on how to survive Armageddon. His vision of the world became steadily bleaker: the use of chemical, atomic and biological weapons would kill off ninety per cent of the world's population. His followers, however, would survive the slaughter because their spiritual practices – using special breathing techniques – would reduce their oxygen intake and make them impervious to the weapons of mass destruction. By 1995, Asahara was predicting that Armageddon could happen at any time. Shortly afterwards, he attempted to launch his own version of the last days of human race.

APOCALYPSE NOW!
Anticipating the End

The last decades of the twentieth century have seen the appearance of cults, sects and churches of every possible persuasion. Most of these movements exist in a state of mutual antipathy, but are united in the belief that an event of momentous importance will occur on

the dawning of the year 2000. One such group is the Aetherius Society, which believes that the world will survive the new millennium because of their prayer energy, which is stored in "radionic" batteries; it will assist the "Cosmic Masters" in guiding humanity after the dawning of the year 2000. The Raelian Movement believes that an embassy must be built in Israel by the year 2030 to welcome the "Elohim," the angels who were responsible for the creation of all human life.

Others are more sinister, like the People's Temple, which introduced the world to the killing fields of salvation. Established by Jim Jones, and eventually located in a remote part of Guyana, this community was convinced that it was under threat from outside forces. Jones had laid down the rule that the community must live or die together, and on 18 November 1978 over nine hundred people followed his orders and either drank or were injected with cyanide.

In April 1993, Waco, Texas, witnessed its own version of "The Last Days," when the Ranch Apocalypse went up in flames, causing the deaths of 86 people. The ranch was the headquarters of a fundamentalist sect called the Branch Davidians, whose leader David Koresh firmly believed that the end of the world was near, and had told his followers that their deaths would be the beginning of their immortal lives.

THE BOOK OF DANIEL
A Threat to European Unity

 Second only to the *Book of Revelation* as the fount of "End Time" knowledge is the Old Testament *Book of Daniel*. It describes the allegorical dream of King Nebuchadnezzar and its interpretation by Daniel: the king dreams of a great image with a head of gold, the breast and arms of silver, the belly and thighs of brass, and the feet part iron and part clay. A stone appears from nowhere and strikes the feet of the image, which break into pieces; the statue crumbles to dust which is blown away, while the stone becomes a great mountain, filling the whole earth (*Daniel*, 2:31–35).

Daniel said that the dream represented the fall of four kingdoms of descending degrees of worth (gold, silver, brass and an iron/clay mix). The use of metals to delineate ages also occurs in Hindu and Greek mythology. The stone in Daniel's vision represents the kingdom of God that will stand forever.

Dr David Yonggi Cho, founder of the Full Gospel Church in Seoul, Korea, has studied the *Book of Daniel* and concluded that the 2000 years of the Gospel Age are about to end. Dr Cho believes the toes of the statue represent the ten nations of the European Community: "Europe is slowly marching towards unity. I believe that when we hear that the unity of ten nations in Europe has been achieved, then the drama of the 'End Time' will speed up dramatically." Some fundamentalist Christians believe that the original ten nations of the European Economic Community represent the ten kingdoms over which the Beast, Anti-Christ, will rule, "I behold a beast, dreadful and terrible, and exceedingly strong...and it had ten horns." (*Daniel*, 7:7). A thought for the politicians of the Old World!

GODS OF THE NEW AGE
Divine Teachings for the Millennium

For many people, the prospect of a new era brings a sense of renewed hope: life will become even better and more advanced for the citizens of planet Earth. Many expect the new millennium to be a time of transformation to a new cosmic cycle, with humanity at the beginning of a path that will lead to a new and more elevated sense of spirituality and meaningful existence on earth. This is because the two-thousand-year period of the Age of Aquarius beckons, and New Age believers think that the turning of the millennial cycles will be the point for the descent from on high of New Gods. These enlightened beings will instruct mankind in new forms of knowledge.

The expectation of the arrival of New Gods stems partly from the belief that the changeover from one zodiacal age to another has always been marked by the arrival of a New World Teacher. Past teachers include Mithras, Zoroaster, Confucius, Krishna, Christ, Buddha and Mohammed, who have all introduced new forms of spirituality and transformed the expectations of large sections of mankind. At the end of the present millennium, the cosmic energy emanating from the constellation of Aquarius, will lead to a new awakening of the human spirit, allowing us to enter new dimensions of development and existence. The New World Teacher will bring the light that will guide humanity out of darkness.

STRANGE IN OUR WORLD
A New Avatar

Buddhist legend recounts that there is a mountain called Meru (often associated with Mount Kailas in Tibet) which represents the Earth revolving on its axis. This sense that mountains are especially holy is widespread in Oriental religions.

Benjamin Creme, the spokesperson for The Lord Maitreya, the new avatar thought to be living in London, England, says that  "gods" still live in the Himalayas, and also in the Andes, Urals, Atlas Mountains and the Rocky Mountains. They are organized in a ritualistic hierarchy, under a "King of the World:" the "Masters of the World," the "Four Veiled Masters," the "Masters of Wisdom," the "Hierarchy of Masters," "The Masters of the Spiritual Hierarchy" and the "Lords of Compassion." Together they are members of "The Great White Brotherhood," otherwise known as "The Society of the Mutant Mind" or "The Elder Brothers of Humanity." They have been watching and superintending the evolution of humanity since the beginning of time.

From the Himalayan mountain stronghold, Creme states, has appeared The Lord Maitreya to act as the new avatar and to guide humanity into a new golden age at the time of the millennium. The Gods have known that they would have to return and be in the midst of humanity at the time of the new cosmic cycle – the Age of Aquarius – when their help will be required to channel the energies of the new age.

FUTURE DISCUSSIONS
Conversations with Nostradamus, Confucius, the Buddha and Jesus

Ryuho Okawa was born on 7 July 1956, and received a degree in law from the University of Tokyo. By the age of 30, he was working as a financial trader for a Japanese company on Wall Street. On 23 March 1981, he received the revelation that he was, in reality, the reincarnation of the Buddha Shakyamuni. This revelation brought him the ability to communicate with the spirit personae of hundreds of prophets and spiritually advanced people, including Nostradamus, Jesus and Confucius.

By October 1986, he had returned to Japan and founded Kofuku-no-Kagaku (The Institute for Research in Human Happiness). The movement is dedicated to purifying and elevating each individual's mind. Its second aim is the creation of a utopia on earth, where all the peoples of the world can live in happiness.

Kofuku-no-Kagaku started with just four members, but by the mid 1990s had grown to an organization of around 300,000 members, with Master Ryuho Okawa as its guru. In 1991, Okawa revealed to his followers that he was the reincarnation of the "Lord El Cantare," the supreme grand spirit of the terrestrial group, who had previously been incarnated as Buddha Shakyamuni and also as Hermes in Ancient Greece. Okawa warned that unless membership of Kofuku-no-Kagaku continues to expand, Mount Fuji could explode. He has also claimed that Japan will become the center of a great East Asian Civilization early in the next millennium.

SACRED MOUNTAINS
Moving to the Roof of the World

Fundamentalist Christians and New Age believers unite in their appreciation of the importance of mountains. The fundamentalists believe that those chosen to be saved by God at the coming of the third millennium, known as the "Elect of God," must make their way to the mountain tops. There they will await an act of divine intervention which will spare them from the horrors of the time leading to the battle of Armageddon. New Age believers also know that the only way to survive the forthcoming millennial earth changes will be to live in the mountains and await the dawning of a new world. It is there the Gods will reveal themselves when the cosmic signs are both propitious and harmonious at the dawning of the Age of Aquarius in the year 2000.

Since time immemorial, the tops of the mountains of the world have evoked a sense of awe and wonder. They are considered to represent everything that is pure, beautiful and pristine; they inspire the on-looker with their loneliness, majesty and absoluteness. Even today, Mount Fuji is not only considered a sacred mountain from the point of view of the Japanese, but also the gateway to another world. In North America, the Blackfoot people of Montana regard Chief Mountain as the home of the Old Man, the first creative force. Mount Kailas, in Tibet, is regarded by Buddhists as a huge natural mandala, the epicenter of powerful Tantric forces. And across religious divides, these places will be the foci of attention in 2000.

THE LORD MAITREYA
The Return of Spiritual Energy

The Lord Maitreya came into public awareness through the messages of Madame Helena Blavatsky (1831–91), a medium and founder of the Theosophical Society. One of her most famous works was *Isis Unveiled*, though she always maintained that the book

had not in fact been written by her, but by three Tibetan Mahatmas: Master Morya, Djwhal Khul and Koot Hoomi. The latter had also informed her that The Lord Maitreya would make himself known at the dawning of the Age of Aquarius.

In June 1945, The Lord Maitreya, leader of the group of "Masters" in the Himalayas, announced his intention of taking his place among suffering humanity. But the nations of the Earth maintained their ways of greed, selfishness and nationalism, and he decided to postpone his return until 1977. In that year, he finally came down from his mountain fastness, first to the plains of Pakistan, then later to London.

In spite of his continued withdrawal from the public eye, The Lord Maitreya has issued guidelines for the salvation of humanity through his spokesperson: "The world belongs to all the people of the planet and the human race must create the conditions for all to live in peace; this can be achieved by the provision of food for everybody, the provision of housing for everybody, the provision of health care for everybody and the provision of education for everybody." But he does warn that if the tensions that are current in the world are not resolved, then there will be a World War III, which will be Armageddon.

THE FALL OF ROME?
Novel Versions of the Catholic Future

The power and influence of the Pope over the followers of Roman Catholicism is without question, but each Pope is always faced with one terrible question: "Am I presiding over the last days of the Church of Rome?"

The fall of the Church of Rome has been traditionally associated with the end of time, as Jesus said to Peter, "Thou art Peter, and upon this rock I will build my church" (*Matthew*, 16:18). And if the rock should vanish, then so will the world.

Several Popes have had terrifying visions of the future, including Pope Pius X (1903–13). During an audience with the General Chapter of the Franciscans in 1909, he experienced a vision: "What I have seen is terrible. The Pope will have to flee the Vatican and leave Rome. He will have to walk over the dead bodies of the priests."

Changes to the state of the Church of Rome, even before the end of this millennium have also been predicted by many seers. Jeane Dixon, America's most famous modern seer and a staunch Roman Catholic, predicted that the Church would experience splits within its ranks over the interpretations of its doctrines and traditions. She also predicted that a Pope would be assassinated before the year 2000, and that the Church would split into many different sects. Nostradamus also forecast many changes within the Church as the year 2000 approaches, including Christian ideals being replaced by Eastern philosophies.

FAMOSO·DOCTOR   PARESELSVS

THE SECOND COMING
A.D. 2000 – The Year of Christ's Return

To the fundamentalist, born-again and evangelical Christian, the Bible not only gives exact and set rules on how to live in this world, but is also an entirely factual account of history from its beginning in 4000 B.C. to the time of the Second Coming of Jesus in A.D. 2000.

History can be divided into time frames of 2000 years each: from Adam, the first man, to Abraham, from Abraham to Jesus, and from Jesus to the year 2000. This view of time was further strengthened by Bishop Hugh Latimer who wrote in 1552, "The world was ordained to endure, as all learned men affirm, 6,000 years. Now of that number there be passed 5,552, so that there is no more left but 448." And now even less – a fact which acts as an inspiration for the fundamentalist Christians as they struggle to get the message of Christ across to the world's non-believers before 2000. They are striving to fulfil the words of *Matthew*, 24: 13–14: "He that shall endure unto the end... shall be saved...This gospel of the kingdom shall be preached in all the world for a witness unto all nations; and then shall the end come."

PAPAL PROPHECY
Jubilation in Rome

In 1995, Pope John Paul II (elected 16 August 1978) indicated in his apostolic letter, "Tertio Millennio Adveniente," ways in which Roman Catholics should prepare to celebrate the year 2000, the Great Jubilee of the Birth of Jesus.

In 1997, all Roman Catholics commence a three-year programme of religious study, firstly devoting themselves to contemplating Jesus and the mystery of salvation. In 1998, they concentrate on the meaning and work of the Holy Spirit, which they believe to be the perfect force created from contemplation of the Son by the Father. In 1999, they undertake a strict course of self-analysis, examining their consciences, recognizing their sins and increasing their use of confession.

The Pope looks forward to the year 2000 and the third millennium as "a new advent for the Church and for humanity." He does not believe the third millennium will be the time of the Apocalypse or Armageddon, but rather the moment when the Church enters a new era of revitalization, and a growth of world-wide spirituality.

He believes that faith and hope will flourish in the future because of the fall of Communism, technological advances, a new concern for the environment and the desire to close the gap between the rich and poor nations of the world. For John Paul, the third millennium is a crucial moment of time perhaps to be marked by "the return of Christ and the Virgin Mary clothed with the sun."

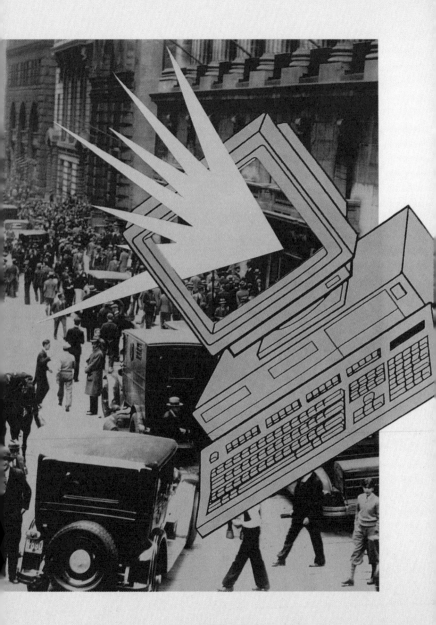

CRASH!
Can the Old Economic Order Survive?

One sentiment which unites such millennial seers and mystics as Edgar Cayce, The Lord Maitreya and Anton LaVey, founder of the contemporary Church of Satan, is their conviction that the present world economic and monetary structures are intrinsically unfair and wrong. The Lord Maitreya, for instance, through his spokesperson, Benjamin Creme, is adamant about the action which needs to be taken by the year 2000: "Market forces are the forces of evil. Any country which follows those forces will end up by being destroyed. We are now seeing the rise of state capitalism, but what is needed is the demise of capitalism. The economic totalitarianism of market forces must be swept aside. When the stock markets of the world collapse, then the priorities of all governments will change, and that will happen in the near future."

In 1990, Marina Tsvygun, a Ukrainian journalist, became convinced that she was the final incarnation of Christ on Earth and changed her name to Maria Devi Christos. She issued a warning to the world about Satan's subversion of the world's economic system through the use of bar codes. Every bar code contains three pairs of thin lines which are slightly longer than the rest of the lines and represent "666," the number of the Beast.

Of more serious concern is the prediction that on 1 January 2000 the world's communications networks will collapse, no aeroplanes will fly, the world's stock markets will go into terminal meltdown, and millions of companies will go out of business. All this will happen because the world's computer systems will simultaneously experience a global crash. They are currently only programmed to use the last two digits of each year. The double zero of the year 2000 will throw them into an immediate state of confusion, because it suggests nothing less than the end of time!

REDUNDANT MONEY
The New Financial Order, Korean Style

The new world that will come into being at the new millennium will also be the start of a Korean golden age. In the opinion of the Ch'ondogyo religious movement, money will be unnecessary because all forms of trade will be carried out by barter; there will be no taxation.

Korea has more than 240 religious movements grouped broadly under the term "New Religions." Their origins can all be traced back to the Tonghak Movement of the 1860s, which was founded as a reaction against the spread of Christianity and Western influence. It took elements of Confucianism, Buddhism and Taoism and combined them into a belief system which emphasized optimism and faith in a better future for Korea. The movement later changed its name to Ch'ondogyo, becoming more a religious/nationalist organization driven by the basic idea that man can attain divine virtue through the cultivation of self-discipline and so influence everything in the outside world without conscious effort.

For the followers of Ch'ondogyo, the cashless paradise will be achieved at the beginning of the new millennium. Everything will be perfect. The weather will never be too cold, too hot, too wet or too dry, and the harvests will, therefore, always be sumptuous. There will be no diseases. Man will live for a minimum of 300 years or, indeed, for ever if he wants. The international language will be Korean! The central site of the new paradise will be Mount Kyeryong, near Taejon City, South Korea, the location of four ancient Buddhist temples and revered throughout Korea. It is thought of as the ideal place because of its potent symbolic form – its ridges look like the scales of a dragon.

THE SATANIC MILITIA
The Individual Versus the State

The view that capitalism and market forces are the forces of evil is endorsed by Anton LaVey. Born on 11 April 1930, of a mixture of French, Hungarian, German, Russian and Rumanian stock, he spent much of his early life traveling from town to town across America. He worked in circuses and carnivals as an animal trainer, musician, magician, hypnotist, and finally as a police photographer. He also appeared as the Devil in the Roman Polanski film, *Rosemary's Baby*.

On Walpurgis Night 1966 he founded the Church of Satan, and published *The Satanic Bible* in 1969. The basic principle of the "church" is "Do what you will," the gratification of the individual through the pursuit of all physical and mental pleasures. In common with many extreme militia groupings, he believes in stern resistance to interference by centralized state institutions and big business: "There is an unrecognized war going on in this country at the moment. It is an economic war. It is being waged by people who have the most money to gain against those with the most to lose. It is the Great Consumer War." The outcome of this war – the collapse of the capitalist system – coincides with the version of breakdown held by many millennial beliefs.

Another American visionary, Edgar Cayce, also saw financial collapse as a kind of metaphor for the chaos awaiting a sinning humanity: "There must surely come a time when there will be panic in the money centers, not only on Wall Street but a closing of banks in many centers and a readjustment of the actual species."

THE SHAWNEE CURSE
A Threat to the American Way of Life

Every American President serves with the knowledge that the curse of the Shawnee may be hanging over him. This malediction, which foresees the premature death of Presidents elected at twenty-year intervals, or at multiples of twenty, was uttered by Chief Tecumseh as he lay dying at the Battle of the Thames, near Detroit, in 1813, after an engagement with soldiers commanded by the then General William Harrison. The curse, which first came into effect when Harrison was elected President in 1841, could be heading for its final and dramatic conclusion with the dawning of the year 2000.

Harrison died two months after becoming President, but the curse then seemed to apply in the cases of Lincoln, Garfield, Harding and Kennedy. It is to be hoped that the curse has become inactive, since the forty-year gap from the election of President Kennedy in 1960 to the beginning of the new millennium could indicate that there is a doubly disastrous event ahead.

THE GREAT STOCK MARKET DISASTER
The Lord Maitreya Foretells the
Collapse of Capitalism

The new millennium will be marked by new energies which are currently waiting to enter our world from the constellation of Aquarius. They represent humanity's last chance to redeem itself, or face total destruction. These energies are very much the concern of the prophecies of The Lord Maitreya, and they hold little comfort for capitalism, which is seen as preventing humanity from living together in a just system. The transformation of the present world order will begin with the fall of the Tokyo stock market: "The market force economy is against the law of evolution because it is not just. The current economic system as expounded by the United States and other Western countries must be swept aside. What is called 'recession' is the beginning of a complete collapse of the current world economic system."

Market forces are the forces of evil, according to The Lord Maitreya, and any people which continues to follow those forces will be destroyed. When the stock markets of the world collapse, then the priorities of all governments will change for the better. These events must come to pass in about the year 2000 to take advantage of the release of Aquarian energies. Otherwise, the tensions which exist between the developing world and the developed world will not be reconciled. The price of continuing global injustice will be World War III.

VII

WATERWORLD
The New Atlantis – the Prophecies of Edgar Cayce

Edgar Cayce (1877-1945), posthumously nominated as "America's Most Mysterious Man" by *House of Mystery* magazine, gained considerable fame as a prophet in pre-war America. Indeed, he still has his followers today, notably among New Age investigators of the Sphinx and the Pyramids. He was also fascinated by the legend of the lost continent of Atlantis and the possiblity of its return.

This legend of a lost golden age, of a time when mankind was cultured, sophisticated and enlightened, has inspired many people who are in despair over our present "evil" age. The story of Atlantis has ancient beginnings; it was Plato who first gave an extended account of legends which had originated in Egypt about a vast empire, beyond the "Pillars of Hercules" (the Straits of Gibraltar) and the Mediterranean, which had met with a catastrophic end. A highly organized state, Atlantis had been a land of civilized amenities, leisure, fine architecture, superb art, plentiful public services and great literature.

On the strength of such descriptions, those people who anticipate the dawning of a New Age have yearned for the return of the lost continent of Atlantis, the land of the Blest, and the year 2000 could be the time when the predictions of Edgar Cayce and his followers will come true, but the Atlanteans known to Cayce are very different from the supremely civilized beings of Plato.

AMERICA'S MOST MYSTERIOUS MAN
Edgar Cayce, the Sleeping Prophet

Born on a farm in a small, isolated rural community, near Hopkinsville, Kentucky, in March 1877, Cayce was a troubled child, but under the influence of his religiously devout mother, he found comfort in the Bible. At the age of six, he discovered that he was able to see and talk to visions, and at seven he had his first contact with "The Universal Mind." He was suddenly confronted by a bright light, while walking in the woods. A voice emanated from the light and asked him what he would like to do with his life. He answered that he wanted to help other people.

On leaving school, Cayce had wanted to be a preacher, but abandoned this ambition when he lost his voice at the age of twenty-one. Desperately seeking a cure, Cayce visited a hypnotist under whose influence he was able to re-enter his boyhood trance state. A strong clear voice came to him, suggesting a remedy. Following this, his throat tissues were restored to full working order. His reputation as an intuitive healer began to spread and, on 9 October 1910, the *New York Times* devoted a two-page article to Cayce and his work.

Under the continuing influence of "The Universal Mind," Cayce predicted the destruction of a large part of the globe by 1998, the advent of World War III in 1999 and the end of our civilization in A.D. 2000. His forecasts for the new millennium are among the most detailed of any futurologist of this century, and global in their significance.

THE DROWNED WORLD
And the Waters
Shall Repossess the Earth

The changes to the planet foreseen by Cayce at the end of the millennium will start with movements along the West Coast of America; Los Angeles and San Francisco will be among the cities to be destroyed. Following this geographical upheaval, new lands will arise in the Caribbean. South America will be so shaken by earthquakes that a new land will emerge between Tierra del Fuego and the Antarctic. Many parts of the East Coast will be affected, in particular the area between New York and Connecticut. New York City will disappear into the sea, and new lands appear off the coast. In the southern part of the United States, large areas of Carolina and Georgia will be submerged. The major part of Japan may disappear under the sea, while northern Europe will change beyond recognition. There will be disturbances in the Arctic and Antarctic, causing volcanoes in Equatorial areas to erupt.

Following such changes, the Earth's poles will shift to such an extent that countries where the climate is arctic will become tropical. All this will happen just before the new millennium. Fortunately, however, there will be some safe areas: Virginia Beach, Ohio, Indiana, Illinois and much of the south and east of Canada.

ATLANTIS RESURGENT
A Continent of Lost Dreams

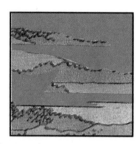

In 1940, Edgar Cayce predicted the return of parts of the lost continent of Atlantis in 1968 or 1969. "Poseida" would be the first part to resurface, in the vicinity of Bimini in the Bahamas. In September 1968, a Bahamian fishing guide brought to the attention of archaeologist Dr J. Manson Valentine, of the Miami Museum of Science, a line of rectangular stones lying in seven metres of water off Paradise Point, Bimini. These stones remain a geological mystery. May we suppose that the re-emergence of Atlanta will be on or around the year 2000 and that it has already begun?

Cayce was fascinated by Atlantis because he thought that it was the site of the original Eden. Man had existed on the earth about ten million years ago, but only in a spiritual and non-physical form; Atlantis was where man changed to his physical form around 200,000 B.C. The Atlantean thought-forms had eventually transformed themselves into five races: white, black, yellow, brown and red. The red race was the true Atlantean race and created a highly developed civilization.

After three periods of self-inflicted destruction between 15,600 B.C. and 10,000 B.C., Atlanteans settled in Europe and North and South America. Evidence of these survivors, Cayce claimed, can be found in the Pyramids, the monuments of Yucatan, and at Bimini. The remnants of the continent sank beneath the Atlantic around 9,700 B.C.

WORLD LIBERATOR
The Return of Edgar Cayce

The insights which Edgar Cayce achieved in his trance states confirmed his belief in reincarnation. After one hypnotic session in Dayton, Ohio, he declared, "A man is born into many different bodies." Later in life, Cayce described his past incarnations as Ra-Ta, an Egyptian priest, and as a soldier in the British army prior to the American War of Independence. In more millennial mode, he believed that he would return as the "world liberator" before the start of World War III in 1999, or that he would definitely be reincarnated in Nebraska in A.D. 2100, obviously having survived the end of the world in A.D. 2000.

In this latter vision, he saw himself returning in a physical body, but with the knowledge that he had been Edgar Cayce and had lived from 1877 to 1945. His return will include a flight across America in a cigar-shaped craft, when he will witness the changes that have happened to the land, and scene after scene of massive devastation and desolation. Upon landing in the endless ruins of a shattered and wrecked city, he will ask, "Where am I?" "New York City," will be the reply.

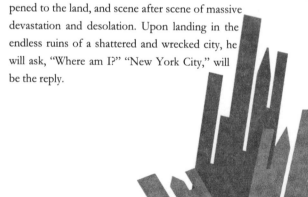

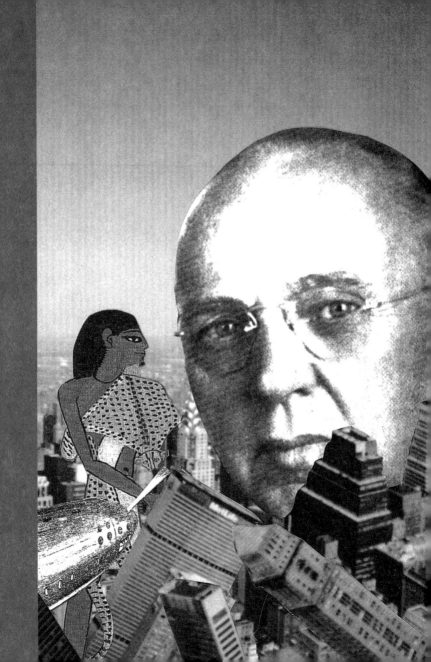

THE MONUMENT WITH A MESSAGE
Readings from the Great Pyramid

The Great Pyramid is not only the world's oldest existing monument, dating from about 2160 B.C., it has also become over the millennia of its existence an ever-growing source of secret messages. Some seers and mystics believe that the Great Pyramid was built by visitors from beyond the stars, who left it behind as a key to the future and as a chamber from which the "aware" could travel through the realms of time and space.

Further evidence of its occult importance is its position on the spot which was regarded as the center of the Earth. It stands equidistant from the two lines of longitude which marked Egypt's ancient borders on the longitude of 30 degrees and on the latitude of 30 degrees which is equidistant from the North Pole and the Equator. The meridian running through the pyramid divides the continents and oceans into two equal halves. While the four sides of the Great Pyramid face due North, South, East and West, and a quarter arc from the center of the pyramid precisely circumscribes the Nile delta.

It also acts as a guide to the universe and points to the places where the "Gods" may live. In 2160 B.C., the Earth was in the constellation of Taurus. The entrance of the Great Pyramid was not only aligned to the equinoctial point which was Alcyone (h Tauri) in the Pleiades, but also to the Northern polar star which in 2160 B.C. was Thuban (a Draconis) in the constellation of the Dragon (Draco). Over the ensuing thousands of years, the pole star has changed. It is now Polaris in Ursa Minor, and the Great Pyramid is today aligned with Polaris. In 2170 B.C. the celestial meridian of the vernal equinox coincided with Tauri, but this stellar combination will not happen again for another 25,700 years, which is approximately the length of time of the procession of the equinoxes.

A MONUMENT TO ETERNITY
Celestial Measurements

Only Egypt can mark her time as the most important country in the known world in terms of millennia, and the Great Pyramid still stands as the ultimate testimony to her period of power, domination and mystery; it is truly a "wonder of the world." Seekers of occult wisdom are certain that it is central to our understanding of the cosmos because it contains so much data about the universe. Twice the vertical height of the Great Pyramid, divided by the area of its base, gives the value of pi = 3.14159 ad infinitum – the key to pure mathematics. Pi is the value of the circumference of a circle in terms of its diameter. The vertical height of the Great Pyramid is the radius of a theoretical circle, the length of the circumference being equal to the sum of the lengths of the four sides of the pyramid.

The density of the great Pyramid is equal to the density of the earth, and the horizontal distance to the vertical axis of the Great Pyramid is 3652.42 pyramid inches which when divided by ten is the number of days of the year. The Great Pyramid also gives the distance from the Earth to the Sun – approximately 93,000,000 miles, – when the height is multiplied by 1,000,000,000 .

Another significant numerological statement is found above the doorway of the King's Chamber, where there are four distinct, parallel lines that descend from the ceiling to the top of the door. They divide the area into five equal spaces, and so make anyone who enters the King's Chamber bow to the number five, the symbol for the human race and the sign of creation.

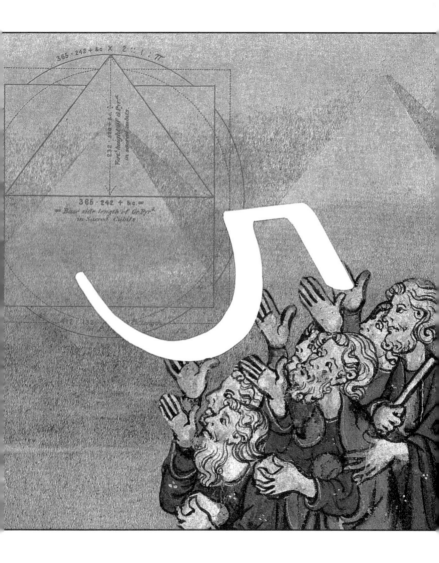

365 · 242 + &c × 2 :: 1 : π

365.242 + &c =
= Base side length of Gt.Pyd.
in Sacred Cubits.

632.999 + &c
Perpendicular of Gt.Pyd.
in sacred cubits.

INSIDE THE PYRAMID
Passages to the Millennium

Piazzi Smyth (1819–1900), Astronomer Royal for Scotland, and author of *The Great Pyramid: Its Secrets and Mysteries Revealed,* declared: "The Great Pyramid is, in its origin and in its nature, a structure of

purity. Its purpose is something entirely different to its perceived use. It represents an archive of hidden knowledge both mathematical and unworldly which was not discovered by the Western world until about three thousand years later. If read correctly, with knowledge of the true length of the sacred cubit – 25.025 British inches – then the pyramid speaks intelligibly, intellectually and religiously to all people."

He likened the descending passage which ends at the pit as the road to hell; the way out of the abyss is via a natural grotto on the descending path which represents the "Paradise of the Dead," in which men can await the final trump of the "Day of Judgment" and return of "The Millennial King." *The Egyptian Book of the Dead* gives additional meaning to this passage, calling it "The Descent" and taking it to represent earthly, material life. The pit is referred to as "The Chamber of Ordeal." The ascending passage to the Grand Gallery is reserved for those souls who choose to embrace Christian belief. The Grand Gallery represents the length of time that humanity has been living under "Christian Dispensation" which precedes the "Second Coming of the Millennial King." To the Egyptians, it was known as the "Hall of Truth in Darkness." The low passage which leads to the King's Chamber represents the "End of the Age."

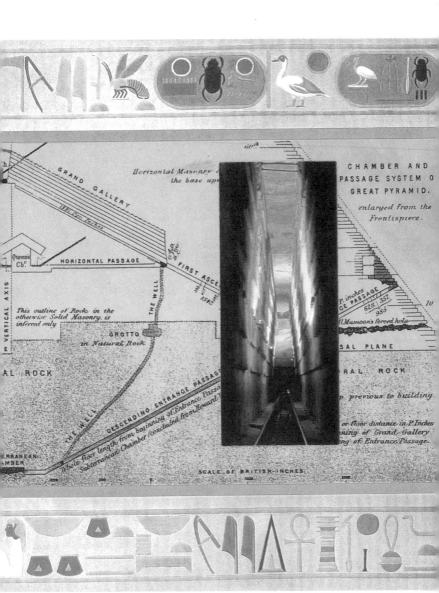

CHAMBER AND
PASSAGE SYSTEM O
GREAT PYRAMID.

*enlarged from the
Frontispiece.*

GRAND GALLERY

Horizontal Masonry
the base up

Queens Ch.ʳ   HORIZONTAL PASSAGE   FIRST ASCE

VERTICAL AXIS

This outline of Rock in the
otherwise Solid Masonry is
inferred only

THE WELL

GROTTO
in Natural Rock

P. inches
CE PASSAGE   628 : 357
935
Mamoon's forced hole

AL ROCK

SAL PLANE

RAL ROCK

w previous to building

DESCENDING ENTRANCE PASSAG

THE WELL

Whole floor length from beginning of Entrance Passa
Subterranean Chamber concluded from Howard

or floor distance in P. Inches
ing of Grand Gallery
ng of Entrance Passage

ERRANEAN
MBER

SCALE OF BRITISH INCHES.

PYRAMIDOLOGY AND CHRISTIANITY
Foretelling the Second Coming

A number of Christian authors have interpreted the Great Pyramid as a cosmic sign of God's divine plan for the Earth. John and Morton Edgar, for instance, authors of *The Great Pyramid Passages*, ascribed specific meanings to the various passages. The passage which descends to the underground chamber symbolizes the downward course of the world since Adam was evicted from the Garden of Eden. The main chamber is the state of death from which only "the saved" can emerge. The ascending passage represents the divine decree granted to the Israelites by God. It symbolizes the blessing of life on earth by God. This time of blessing is believed to have started with the exodus of the Israelites from Egypt in about 1615 B.C., and ended with the crucifixion of Jesus in A.D. 33. The Grand Gallery indicates the coming of Jesus. The passage to the Queen's Chamber denotes perfect human life and nature at the end of Christ's millennial reign, and also shows the potential for eternal life. The antechamber to the King's Chamber signifies the school of Christ, while the King's Chamber shows the inheritance of immortality by those who possess a divine nature and have joined with God. Within the King's Chamber is the empty coffer, and its measurements are the same as those of the Ark of the Covenant.

In *The Great Pyramid: Its Time Features*, Morton Edgar takes the length of the Grand Gallery (1,915 pyramid inches) to represent the date on which Jesus Christ would return as the invisible ruler of the world for 1,000 years. This would then make the date for the end of the world A.D. 2914. It also means that the millennial Messiah is already among us.

THE MESSAGE IN THE STONES
The Pyramid and the Messiah

The power and majesty of the Great Pyramid are awesome; its stones, passage-ways and chambers have inspired countless New Age prophets to comment on the end of this millenium and the prospects for a new beginning – or end! The train of their deductions has frequently been obscure, but the final message has usually been uncompromising.

From information enshrined in the Great Pyramid, the Mexican seer, Rudolfo Benavides forecast in 1961 that a world cataclysm would occur before the end of this millennium. The world would shift on its axis, causing the ice-caps to melt and the oceans to rise by sixty feet. The world's climate would also change to one of continuous rainfall. He predicted that by 2001 about seventy per cent of the world's population would have been wiped out.

A later Pyramid prophet, Max Toth, predicted in 1979 that a series of natural disasters would occur in the 1990s, again including a massive shift in the earth's axis. New lands will rise from the sea, while once familiar countries will sink beneath the waves. The climate will continue to deteriorate, with incessant volcanic eruptions, continuous earthquakes and violent storms. Civilization as we know it will continue to decline and finally break down in 2025.

But Toth sees Messianic hope in the messages from the Great Pyramid. Following the collapse of our civilization a new world order of great spirituality will be established. In 2040, the Messsiah will return in a physical body, and the period between 2055 and 2115 will be a golden age for humanity, which will grow in prosperity and spiritual consciousness. In 2116 the Messiah will pass away, but be reincarnated in 2135 and again in 2265.

TO WALK AMONG THE STARS
A Giant Leap for Mankind

As the centuries have ticked away, the discoveries and experiences that our planet has to offer have shrunk to such an extent that it is now known as the "global village." In short, the planet can no longer provide the horizons and inspirations that are needed for people to get the most out of life. One reaction to current human frustration is the turning to extreme and fundamentalist religious beliefs which are unforgiving in their attitude to any alternative form of faith. Rigid in their doctrine that only believers can be saved from eternal damnation, many such cults do foresee the final destruction of the world in the year 2000. Even gentler and more tolerant seers and mystics who have forecast that the coming of the Age of Aquarius will usher in a New Age believe that something very significant is going to happen at the coming of the new millennium. The downside of both these positions is that they anticipate the deaths of many millions before the concept of a new world, of whichever nature, can be put into effect.

It is undeniable that at the year 2000 mankind will be at a momentous point in history – very few generations have had the opportunity to stand at the point of a metaphysical zero and contemplate a new age beginning. Must we then bury our heads in the sands of superstition and religious bigotry? Or do we face the future head on and take the next steps into the universe to walk among the stars?

2001 – AN ODYSSEY
Space is the Place

On 20 July 1969, Neil Armstrong uttered what would become one of the most famous sentences in the world: "That's one small step for man, one giant leap for mankind." And, at that moment, he fulfilled the dreams of countless numbers of people from across the millennia: man had set foot on the surface of another world and unlocked the door to the future.

In other words, space is the place for the human race, but since that glorious day of the Moon walk, extraterrestrial programs have had to struggle to survive in the face of severe budgetary restrictions from governments displaying a significant lack of foresight and imagination about the future of this planet and its people.

The original vision expressed by Professor Gerard O'Neill at the second General Assembly of the World Future Society in 1975 ("The human race stands on the threshold of a new frontier whose riches are a thousand times greater than that of the new Western World of 500 years ago.") seems to have been clouded. The plans for solar-powered satellites to beam electrical energy to the Earth and make redundant our dependence on fossil fuels lie in abeyance, while projects for colonies for mining the ores of the Moon and the asteroids remain in the realm of science fiction.

The year 2000 brings a new age to the human race, and a new age demands a new resolution. It is, therefore, surely time to leave behind the constraints of our earthbound perspective and set out determinedly, for the benefit of all mankind, to explore the new frontiers and so discover our true place in the universe.

THE MUSIC OF THE SPHERES
Is There Anybody Out There?

If we knew for certain that we were not alone in the universe, every part of our world view and every aspect of our lives would be fundamentally changed. Today, it is estimated that our galaxy, the Milky Way, contains some 250 billion stars, and the universe around 100 billion galaxies. It seems almost inconceivable that we are alone in a gigantic lifeless universe, but physical evidence for any form of planetary life anywhere else in any galaxy is non-existent; no certain conclusions have yet been drawn from the "fossils" from Mars.

However, the theory that our nine planets were formed from the dust and gas resulting from the birth of the Sun could hold true for other star systems. More than thirty years ago, the American astronomer, Frank Drake, calculated that there are approximately forty billion stars in the Milky Way which are similar to the Sun, and he speculated that most of these stars are orbited by at least one planet, of which he reckoned ten per cent could be suitable for life. It is hard to believe that the Earth should be the only planet out of four billion to sustain life.

There is, however, expectation stirring in the scientific community that other life will be found in our own solar system in the not too distant future. The hopes of exobiologists are pinned on the icy Jovian moon, Europa, whose oceans could contain "the primeval soup of life." The present Galileo fly-past may very well yield evidence that we will not be alone in the new millennium.

INTERSTELLAR SUPERCHARGE
Mars in a Month!

Space appears to be densely populated by stars, but the reality is that the distances between the stars are immense and filled with nothing but hydrogen. This poses a problem for all interstellar travellers – how to cover the huge distances. The propulsion systems that are used for our current space transports are simply too inefficient, but the first step on the path to interstellar travel is scheduled to occur in 1997 with the use of an ion thruster on the Artemis communications satellite currently being built by the European Space Agency (ESA). If it is successful, it could be used for space probes and for manned missions to the other planets.

The thruster takes the electrons from gas atoms, and by the use of a powerful electrical field accelerates them to a very high velocity. They are then forced through the thruster in the same way that exhaust gases leave conventional spacecraft. The ions can be accelerated to a much higher velocity and can be run continuously which means that the much higher speeds needed to explore the solar system can be achieved. For example, it is forecast that with an ion thruster the time to Mars would be cut from a year to a month.

Time is long, though ours is short and should be used wisely. In his *Story of Mankind*, Hendrik van Loon invokes a telling image of our place in the great order of the universe: in a faraway place on Earth stands a rock, one hundred miles high, one hundred miles wide; once every thousand years, a bird comes to sharpen its beak on it; when that rock is completely worn away, then a single day of eternity will have passed. In the meantime, it is up to us to see that the year 2000 becomes a gateway to a better future.

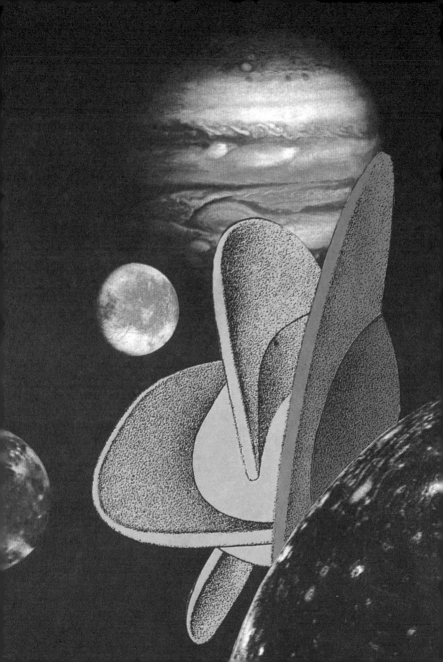

Select Bibliography

Cheetham, Erika, *The Prophecies of Nostradamus*, London, 1973, *The Further Prophecies of Nostradamus*, London, 1985, *The Final Prophecies of Nostradamus*, London, 1990

Cho, Yonggi, David, *Daniel: Insight on the Life and Dreams of the Prophet from Babylon*, London, 1990, *Revolution: Visions of our Ultimate Victory in Christ*, London, 1991

Davidson, D., & Aldersmith, H., *The Great Pyramid: Its Divine Message*, London, 1925

Dixon, Jeane & Noorbergen, Rene, *Jeane Dixon: My Life and Prophecies*, New York, 1970

Fisher, Joe & Cummins, Peter, *Predictions*, London, 1981

Gattey, Neilson Charles, *Prophecy and Prediction*, London, 1989

Hall, Alan, *Nostradamus and Visions of the Future*, Leicester, 1993

Hall, Angus & King, Francis, *Mysteries of Prediction*, London, 1975

Harpur, James & Westwood, Jennifer, *The Atlas of Legendary Places*, London, 1989

Hogue, John & Striker, Carmen, *The Nostradamus Astrological Date Book 1990*, London, 1989

Mann, A.T., *Millennium Prophecies*, London, 1992

McClure, Kevin, *The Evidence for Visions of the Virgin Mary*, London, 1983

Montgomery, Ruth & Gariand, Joanne, *Ruth Montgomery, Herald of the New Age*, New York, 1986

Moore, Patrick, *Countdown*, London, 1983

Petrisko, Thomas W., *Call of the Ages*, Santa Barbara, 1995

Rabanne, Paco, *Has The Countdown Begun?*, London, 1994

Roberts, Henry C., *The Complete Prophecies of Nostradamus*, New York, 1947

Rudaux, Lucien & De Vaucouleurs, G., *Larousse Encyclopedia of Astronomy*, London, 1966

Smyth, Piazzi, *The Great Pyramid, Its Secrets and Mysteries Revealed* (reprint), New York, 1990

Storm, Stella, *Philosophy of Silver Birch*, London, 1969

Storr, Anthony, *Feet of Clay*, London, 1996

Timms, Moira, *Prophecies to Take You into the Twenty-First Century*, London, 1996

Thornton, Penny, *Divine Encounters*, London, 1991

Thompson, Damian, *The End of Time*, London, 1996

Toth, Max, *Pyramid Prophecies*, New York, 1979

Van Loon, Hendrik, *The Story of Mankind*, London, 1962

Wilson, Colin, *The Occult*, London, 1971

Sources of the illustrations

b = bottom, bg = background, c = centre, l = left, r = right

Bank of England 95; © Michael Banks 12, 13cr&l; courtesy, Museum of Fine Arts, Boston 111bg; Tessa Campbell 109b; Peter Clark 25cl, 75bg, 81bg; E.P. Curtis 65r; Graham Harrison 33; © Jim Henderson AMPA 117bg; *North American Indian Designs* by E. Wilson (1984) 25c, 65c, 96–97; A.F. Kersting 61al, 89bg; Anton LaVey 95c; Imperial War Museum, London 44bg&l, 59bg; McDonnell Aircraft Corporation 19bg; Niall McInerney 23c; NASA 13, 16–17, 53, 65, 123, 127; Popperfoto/Reuters 61br, 69, 71, 89bc, 99; Emil Schultess 13bg, 104bg; Alberto Siliotti 115c; Edwin Smith 50–51; Karl Taube 25bg, 38, 391; UPI/Corbis/Bettmann 47c, 91; I.W. Whimster 55ac.